I have a very special friend.
He is called Jesus.

1

Many years ago, Jesus came
to earth as a tiny baby.

My Friend Jesus

By Juliet David

Illustrated By Helen Prole

CANDLE
BOOKS

God gave Jesus a mother called Mary.

3

When Jesus was born, Mary wrapped
him in warm clothes and laid him
in the straw.

5

Jesus grew up like other boys.
He was happy when he played.

And he was sad when friends
were unkind to him.

But Jesus was different from everyone else.

We sometimes do bad things – but he never did. 9

 **10**

When Jesus grew up, he visited little villages and big cities.

Many people followed him.

11

He taught people how to please God.

And how to live together
without hurting one another.

14

One day, lots of people came to hear Jesus. A boy brought his lunch of bread and fish to Jesus.

Jesus broke it into pieces.
There was enough for everyone.

15

16 Another day a crowd of children came to Jesus.

He reached out his arms to them.

17

18 But not everyone loved Jesus.
Bad men nailed Jesus to a cross.

Jesus had done nothing wrong.
His friends were very sad.

19

Jesus died for all the bad things we have done. But three days later, he came back alive! He met his friends again.

21

Jesus went to be with
Father God in heaven.

23

But Jesus is coming back again!

24

If we love Jesus, we will
live with him in heaven
forever!

25

Jesus is my special friend.